THE FACTS ABOUT TEEN SUICIDE

BY

Gail Stewart

EDITED BY

Maythee Kantar

PUBLISHED BY
CRESTWOOD HOUSE
Mankato, MN, U.S.A.

CIP

LIBRARY OF CONGRESS CATALOGING IN PUBLICATION DATA

Stewart, Gail
Teen suicide

(Facts about)
Includes index.
SUMMARY: Describes some of the feelings experienced by teenagers thinking about suicide, the reactions of family members, various reasons for suicide, and the seven warning signs to look for in a person contemplating suicide.
1. Teenagers — United States — Suicidal behavior — Juvenile literature. 2. Suicide — United States — Prevention — Juvenile literature. [1. Suicide.] I. Title. II. Series.
HV6546.S78 1988 362.2—dc19 88-20281
ISBN 0-89686-413-8

International Standard Book Number:
0-89686-413-8

Library of Congress Catalog Card Number:
88-20281

PHOTO CREDITS

Cover: Taurus Photos: Patricia Myers
Taurus Photos: (Pam Hasegawa) 21; (L.L.T. Rhodes) 25
Viewfinders: (Chris Grajczyk) 4, 7, 11, 12, 19, 20, 32; (Tony Koski) 8; (Doug Beasley) 22-23
Third Coast Stock Source: (MacDonald Photography) 14, 38; (Ken Dufault) 17, 30, 36-37, 41; (Todd S. Dacqulsto) 26-27; (William Meyer) 28; (J. P. Slater) 34; (Jack Hamilton) 43

Produced by Carnival Enterprises.

CRESTWOOD HOUSE

Box 3427, Mankato, MN, U.S.A. 56002

TABLE OF CONTENTS

A person's suicide is hard to understand and difficult to accept.

BILL

As Bill walked into the cemetery, the sun was just coming up. A few robins were making a racket in the trees. It was going to be a beautiful May morning.

Bill felt different than he had in weeks, maybe months. It was a peaceful feeling, as though he were finished with the problems that had bothered him since his parents' divorce.

He thought about his mother and his father, and how they had fought. Bill had lain in bed at night trying to block out their angry words. It never really worked, though. He could hear them fighting and calling each other names. It was a relief, at first, when they had finally gotten the divorce.

But the divorce had meant moving to a new neighborhood and a new school. Making friends had never been easy for Bill, but he had had a few friends at his old school. Now it seemed as though everyone had a group of other kids to hang out with except him. It was suddenly hard to talk to these strangers, these kids who fit in so well. He was just the new kid—the one who sat alone at lunch.

As the days went by, Bill found himself feeling tired and bored. He had grown used to being alone. He did his schoolwork without caring if it was right or wrong. He didn't concentrate in class, and except for Mrs. Casey, his math teacher, no one seemed to notice. She had seen that Bill was lonely—she'd even tried to start up a conversation with him in the hall. But Bill just withdrew inside himself, and Mrs. Casey walked away.

When he came home each afternoon, his mother was at work, so he was alone there, too. That was fine with him—he had nothing to say to anybody. He spent most of his time sleeping.

The sky was pink now. Bill sat in the cemetery, leaning against a tombstone. A brown and black shotgun lay in his lap. He felt that this was the answer. By shooting himself, he would be finished with the lonely lunches in the cafeteria at school. He would be done with the invisible days, with the hopelessness he felt.

Nothing is as difficult to understand as a suicide. When it is a teenager who kills himself or herself, it is especially troubling. People who knew the person ask themselves why. How could that young person take his own life? What was so terrible that the only solution was suicide?

Often the victim's family feels shame or guilt, so they don't often talk about it. Half-truths and rumors replace straight talk and open discussion. When this happens, other teens may become frightened and confused about problems in their own lives. Some even identify with the suicide victim, feeling that what "worked" for that person might be the answer for them, as well.

Facts about teen suicide are important for many reasons. If we know the extent of teen suicide in the United States, it can help us focus on ways to help young people in trouble. By knowing the warning signs of suicide, the family and friends of a depressed or angry teen can see when a problem is out of control.

ATTITUDES ABOUT SUICIDE

Historians know there have been suicides for thousands of years. There is a famous illustration

The "epidemic" of teen suicide affects all types of people.

from ancient Egypt that shows a young man thinking about ending his own life. That picture was drawn more than 4,000 years ago! In those times, too, the idea of suicide was frightening to most people. They believed in life after death, and weren't sure whether the soul of a suicide victim would be allowed to enter the afterlife.

In ancient Greece, suicide was viewed as a negative solution to an unhappy life. There was a law in Athens, one of the largest cities in Greece, that the body of a suicide victim had to be buried outside the city limits. Before burial, the victim's hand was cut off and had to be buried separately. The Greeks felt there were really two forces involved in the act of suicide—

the body and the hand that committed murder against it.

People's attitudes about suicide have not always been negative, however. In fact, in some cultures, killing oneself was considered an act of bravery or even a duty!

In Japan, for example, young boys were once trained in the ceremony of *hara-kiri* (pronounced har-i-kir-ē) or "stomach-cutting." This was a form of suicide used when dishonor had been earned, in battle or otherwise. Hara-kiri was common for thousands of years. At the end of World War II, many Japanese officers committed hara-kiri rather than surrender.

Another culture that once encouraged suicide was the Hindu society in India. When a man died, his wife was supposed to throw herself on the funeral fire or drown herself in the Ganges River. The idea of this custom, called *suttee* (pronounced se-tē), was that the woman's death might make up for her husband's sins, and he would be admitted to paradise.

In the Fiji Islands, where men usually had several wives, there was another suicide custom. Like suttee, it was geared only toward women. When an important man in the tribe died, each of his wives hurried to be the first to kill herself. They believed the one who died first would be the man's favorite in the afterlife.

But in the world today, suicide—especially teen suicide—is not thought of as an honor or a duty. It is

By knowing the warning signs of suicide, the family and friends of a depressed teen can help before it is too late.

a frightening problem that isn't going away.

A NATIONAL EPIDEMIC

In the United States, suicide is the second leading cause of death for teenagers. Only accidents claim more lives each year. In 1987, there were more than 600,000 suicide attempts. Six thousand of these ended in deaths. That averages out to about 16 dead teenagers every day.

The national suicide rate is increasing every year. Between 1972 and 1978, the suicide rate for teenagers doubled. There are no signs that it is slowing down. One *psychiatrist* (a doctor who deals with emotional problems) calls the teen suicide rate in this country "a national epidemic."

"It's frightening to all of us," she says, "but especially to those of us with teenagers of our own. The epidemic affects rich, poor, black, white, everybody. It's so dangerous for these kids, and many of them are so confused. No one seems to be taking the time to listen to them."

Many psychiatrists and counselors feel that the 6,000-per-year figure is actually low. Many suicide deaths are explained away as "accidents" to avoid pain and embarrassment for the family. The annual suicide figure does not account for the many teens

Suicide is the second leading cause of death for American teenagers.

who self-destruct through eating disorders, by drug and alcohol use, or by reckless driving.

THE BIG QUESTION

Whenever someone takes his or her own life, the first question asked is "Why?" Why was she so unhappy? Why didn't he tell us he felt lonely? Why did she do something so drastic? When the suicide victim is a teenager, the "why's" are even more confusing.

Adults tend to think back on their own teenage

In 1987, there were 600,000 suicide attempts.

years with happiness. They have memories of dances and football games. They shake their heads in amazement that teens of today complain of depression and stress. Aren't the teenage years supposed to be the best, the most carefree? Aren't they the stuff memories are made of? How could anyone in the prime of life—with so much to look forward to—end it all?

A CHANGING WORLD

Memories often tend to smooth out the rough edges. People remember the fun of childhood, but sometimes they forget the painful moments and the sad times. Lots of adults will say, "Gee, I'd love to be 15 again," but if they were to think seriously about it, they might change their minds! Life as a teenager, they will admit, was more than proms and cheerleading.

Adolescence, the age between childhood and adulthood, is a very difficult time. Teenagers, sometimes called adolescents, are neither children nor adults. In body they look like young women and men, but their emotions don't always keep up. With physical changes come new feelings, some of them difficult to sort out. As one 16-year-old girl puts it, "Half the time your parents are yelling at you to grow up and the other half they treat you like a baby. I don't even know who I am yet—how can they know?"

Also, there are things that make these days a very hard time to be a teenager—harder even than 20 years ago. *Father Knows Best* was a very popular television show in the early '60s. The television family was always shown sitting around a dinner table, calmly discussing various problems of the three children. As the show's name suggests, the answers to the kids' troubles were always found—usually by Father—and life rolled smoothly on. Mother was always home. Father came home at the same time every day. Routine and consistency were the backbone of that family!

As heartwarming as that family life might have been, it is a thing of the past. Families today are on the move. Many families are headed by single parents, and many more by two working parents. With school, work, and recreational schedules colliding, there is often no set time for parents and children to touch base with one another. "I feel guilty sometimes," one mother from Chicago admits. "I have been working four days a week since my husband and I separated. I don't even see my kids on Tuesdays and Wednesdays, except to say 'Are you almost through in the bathroom?' I know they are old enough to be on their own sometimes, but I feel like I'm not paying enough attention. If I don't work, though, we don't eat. I guess we've got to be flexible."

Another reason growing up these days is tough is

Family members need to take some time out of their busy schedules to talk with each other.

the easy access teens have to drugs and alcohol. Add to that a lot of unsupervised free time, and it's easy to see why some teenagers might make some very wrong choices.

NO ONE REASON

Despite the fact that growing up can be very hard, however, most teenagers get through those years without many scars. Certainly there are times of feeling confused or pressured or frightened. That's part of life, for adults as well as for teens. But those feelings eventually pass. Why then, do some young people not make it?

Psychologists, or people who study the ways we act and behave, say that there is no such thing as a typical suicidal teen. "It's not like chemistry, where we could look at something in a test tube and say 'See that thing there—that germ? That germ caused the suicide,' " says one psychologist who works with teens every day. "It would be a lot easier if we could isolate one factor, one horrible thing that causes kids to hurt themselves. Then we could know in advance which kids would need help. Sadly, though, that's just not the case."

In fact, if there's any one thing psychologists do know about the causes of teen suicide, it's that each teen is completely different. There is no single event that would cause most troubled teenagers to commit suicide. Instead, it is the way a teenager reacts to an event that could spell disaster. For one teen, it could be the death of a pet. For another, it would be not making the basketball team. One 14-year-old boy tried to kill himself after learning he had to have braces on his teeth. It would be foolish to think that any one of these reasons alone turned a teenager into a suicide victim. In most cases, it was simply the straw that broke the camel's back.

AT RISK

Psychologists sometimes talk about young people being in an "at-risk" category. That means there are some emotions that can create a dangerous mixture of feelings. Such a mixture could be set off by a series of painful events to produce a suicidal teen.

Anger, guilt, and a feeling of being abandoned are painful feelings, and can put a young person into an at-risk category. A teen whose parents have divorced is quite often bombarded by such feelings. She might be angry at her parents because the divorce disrupts the family. She may have to move away from friends and her school. She probably feels anger at her own helplessness in the situation. Nothing she can do or say really makes much of a difference.

Guilt is also evident in a divorce. There is the nagging feeling that maybe she was at fault for her parents' arguing. Maybe if she had been better, or nicer, or had helped more around the house, her parents wouldn't have gotten divorced.

There are some parents, too, who "use" the child in their bickering. Often one parent will try to get the child's support by saying mean things about the other parent. The child often feels like the rope in a tug of war—being pulled one way and the other, back and forth.

One boy who attempted suicide at the age of 12 remembers with bitterness how he felt when his parents were going through a divorce. "They never really asked me how I felt. I stayed with my mom, and she cried all the time. I needed her to tell me that everything was going to be okay. But she just stayed

At one time or another, everyone feels anger, guilt, or a feeling of being abandoned.

in her room and cried, or else she'd say, 'How can you still love your father after what he's done to us?' I felt like I was a traitor because I still loved him. I was really mixed up."

LOSING YOUR CENTER

All of us need to depend on someone or something. We may count on our parents' love or the respect of our friends. We may even count on ourselves to act in a particular way in a given situation. Some psychologists call this a *center.* Our centers are extremely important, for they act like an anchor in our lives. If things get confusing, we know we can always rely on our center.

In the case of a divorce, a child may lose his or her center for a time. The love and understanding he counted on are suddenly taken away. At the time a child needs love and reassurance the most, it is not there. Parents who, under normal circumstances, are caring and open find that with the stress of a divorce there is no energy left for anyone else. For the parent, the anguish passes after a time and life goes on. The child, unfortunately, often carries the feelings of guilt and anger a long time.

In some cases, a divorce might mean the child and a parent move. A move signals still another loss—this time that of familiar surroundings, friends, school.

Teens need their parents' love or a friend's support to maintain a strong "center."

For many teens, the *peer group*—those friends of the same age—are part of the center. The peer group is part of the support system a teen needs, especially in this difficult time.

"It was the hardest thing I ever had to do," says a 15-year-old from Boston. "We moved here from California. Back there I was an A student and a basketball player. All I kept thinking was—what will I be in Boston?"

There were large numbers of teen suicides in Plano, Texas, in 1983. Plano, a suburb of Dallas, had gone through a period of rapid growth—in ten years the population jumped almost 900%. Some psychologists

Peer groups offer support for teens, especially during difficult times.

feel that many of the suicide victims had lost their centers. Judie Smith, an expert on teen suicide, says, "The common thread is the experience of loss. These kids have lost friendships, ties—it's a traumatic upheaval when a child is moved from one community to another. And once they get through this and there's another loss, like the breakup of a relationship with a boyfriend or girlfriend, it's an added crisis."

THE TUNNEL

Some teens who have attempted suicide say later that they felt terribly empty. Like Bill, the boy who was thinking about suicide at the beginning of this book, they had feelings of being completely alone—even invisible. When most people get sad or depressed, they realize that the feelings will pass. The next day or two, they know, will bring better times and fresh opportunities. But the at-risk teenager sees his life as a long, dark tunnel. There is no light at the end, no glimmer of hope. There are no choices—just darkness. This is despair, or hopelessness. A person without hope has given up. He feels that whatever he does won't make a bit of difference.

When a teen feels like this, he may show it in a number of ways. Often he may stop caring about how he looks—whether his teeth are brushed, or his hair is combed. His appetite may disappear, and he may

Most people realize their sad or depressed feelings will pass in a day or two.

An "at-risk" teenager sees no hope for the future and thinks there are no choices left.

sleep a lot more than normal. But some teens can *mask* or cover up, their despair. They find it hard to communicate the emptiness and depression they feel, and they hide it. They may be star athletes, honor roll students, talented musicians. They may even be in the center of an active social life. But these are masks. They are attempts to forget emptiness by filling time. They only disguise the pain. They don't make it go away.

LOW SELF-ESTEEM

Self-esteem is how we think of ourselves. We learn a lot about ourselves from the people around us, especially family. It's healthy to like ourselves, to respect ourselves. Parents that encourage and listen to their children help build high self-esteem. On the other hand, a child who is criticized or laughed at grows up believing he or she is worth very little.

Most at-risk teens have low self-esteem for a variety of reasons. Sometimes the low self-esteem is accompanied by strong feelings of hatred for themselves. One girl who tried to kill herself when she was 13 was always the target of teasing. "I was a fat little kid. Everybody at school, and even my brothers, used to call me names. I was always the one who got picked last. I never felt good about who I was, even when I did okay on a test. Being fat was who I was."

Some teens create a "mask" that hides their problems instead of solving them.

Some teens acquire low self-esteem from teasing remarks from classmates or even family members.

When she was 12, she began starving herself. She felt that the only way she could become likable was to be thin. This on-purpose starvation is called *anorexia nervosa,* and it is another cry for help from

an at-risk young person. Quite often anorectic teens admit that they acquired their low self-esteem at school from classmates, even from careless remarks made by teachers.

CONDITIONAL LOVE

School is the work of teens. It takes up a good deal of their time and energy. If a young person does well in classes, makes the swim team, or has lots of friends, he or she is considered a "success." Unfortunately, school offers lots of opportunities for failure, too.

If a class is difficult, or if a teen doesn't make the lead in the class play, he or she may feel like a failure, a loser. Even more dangerous, the teen's parents may treat him or her as a failure. Such negative thoughts from parents—a teen's center—can make a teen anxious and fearful of failing again. Self-esteem sinks lower and lower.

Having a healthy self-esteem means feeling good about yourself and knowing that you can resolve problems.

Parents who seem to offer love and kindness only when a teen is "successful" are said to be showing *conditional love.* Although they may not realize the stress they are putting their child under, the message gets through loud and clear. "I'll love you if you make the honor roll; I'll love you if you are invited to the prom; I'll love you if you get into a good college."

Of course, conditional love is not really love at all. It creates fear and pressure for the teen. It does great damage to a young person's self-esteem. It closes off valuable channels of communication—the key to a healthy family life.

THE SUICIDE BELT AND EXAMINATION HELL

Most parents want their children to do well in school. But some parents go too far in their expectations. In a number of ways, they let the child know that they will be greatly disappointed—or even angry—if the child doesn't achieve success.

Sometimes parents do this because they themselves were not capable of getting good grades all the time. In a way, these parents are trying to relive their lives through their children. In other cases, the parents are high achievers—often wealthy and successful in their

Some teens are pressured by their parents to succeed in schoolwork or in sports.

own lives. Such parents may feel that a child who achieves less than perfection would reflect poorly on them. The result of such pressure is often tragic.

Chicago's North Shore, an area of many beautiful homes and wealthy people, has been referred to as the "Suicide Belt." In one period of less than 18 months, 28 teenagers there killed themselves. Psychologists believe many of the teens simply couldn't handle the pressure. "They were told they had to reproduce what their parents had done," says a Chicago psychiatrist. "The child just said, 'I can't. I give up.'"

The United States is not the only country that is having an epidemic of teen suicides. The Japanese school system is far more stressful than that of the U.S., and Japanese teens are killing themselves at an alarming rate.

In Japanese society there is only one way to achieve success, and that is to do well in school. The best positions in business and industry go to the most promising college graduates. The colleges are very careful about which young people they admit. Usually the best high schools produce the best college material. To get into a good high school, students attend high-powered elementary schools. Students advance through their school years strictly on the basis of hard tests, called examinations. Even preschool children are told they ought to begin drilling for important kindergarten examinations! It's not surprising that these testing periods are called "Examination Hells."

If a Japanese teen doesn't do well enough on an examination to proceed to the next level, it is considered a disgrace. The young person feels he or she has brought shame and dishonor upon his or her family. These intense feelings of self-hate and worthlessness have resulted in many suicides.

"THEY'LL BE SORRY"

One thought that often goes through a suicidal teen's mind is getting back at those who made his life miserable. He may fantasize about family and classmates crying over his body when he dies. He may get a lot of satisfaction from these thoughts, although they show that he is not thinking clearly. In his daydreams, he imagines he will be there to enjoy his funeral. He gets pleasure out of the dream of revenge his suicide will bring. He doesn't think about—or perhaps he doesn't know—what "dead" really means.

Psychiatrists say that the "glamorizing" of death is

Many teens who think about their death do not realize death is a final step.

dangerous to at-risk teenagers. To a troubled teen like Bill, who feels invisible, the thought of being an instant celebrity might be appealing. Many high schools have memorial services for suicide victims, and dismiss classes for a day in honor of a dead teen. This practice is alarming to those who work with suicidal teens, for they say that such services tend to make heroes out of the victims. By honoring them in that way, it could very easily encourage other at-risk teens to do the same thing. They could be heroes, too—if not in life, then certainly in death.

Some schools have taken an aggressive approach to wiping out the glamour of death. The point is that if teens understand the grim finality of death, the "they'll be sorry" idea will be less common. Such schools have used films about death, showing what happens after a person dies, the autopsy, and the way the body is prepared for burial. Films like these remove the fantasy and mystery surrounding death.

MYTHS

Suicide has been a topic that most people avoid talking about, and over the years myths have replaced facts about suicide. Such wrong ideas only make understanding a suicide, or an at-risk teen, that much more difficult.

One myth is that anyone who would attempt to commit suicide is crazy. This is certainly not true, but it can be a very damaging idea to the teen who has been troubled or at-risk. Hopelessness and despair are feelings that many of these teens have, and to be thought of as crazy only adds to their problems.

Another myth is that any teen who commits suicide must have had terrible parents. This is unfair; most parents of suicide victims cared about their children

By talking to one another, family members can relieve some of the stress and pressure of everyday life.

very much. It is true that in many cases, the family had trouble communicating. Many of these parents had some difficulty in showing their love and support. Stress and pressure caused by family problems often causes a teen to be at-risk.

One very dangerous belief about suicide is that anyone who talks about committing suicide wouldn't really do it. Not true! What makes this belief so dangerous, in fact, is that a teenager talking to friends or family about his or her own death might not be taken seriously. Quite often, anyone who mentions suicide is extremely troubled, and is, in a way, asking for help. To treat this young person as if he or she is just "trying to get attention" could be a disastrous mistake.

BETTER MAD THAN DEAD

What, then, do you do if a friend tells you that he is thinking about ending his life? What if he swears you to secrecy? This happened to Charlie, a 15-year-old boy from Seattle.

"My friend Mike had been acting strange for about three weeks. I kept going over to his house, but he never wanted to do anything—just hang around at home. Then one day he told me that he had a present

A person who talks about committing suicide is usually not kidding; he or she needs to talk to an adult.

SHELDON

for me. It was his baseball card collection—his prize possession.

"I couldn't figure it out. He'd been collecting for eight years—we both had. Some of them were worth some money. I asked him why; I said, 'I can't take these, Mike.'

"He told me he wasn't going to need them any more. He didn't want to talk about it, but I got this really creepy feeling that he was going to kill himself."

Charlie asked his friend if he was serious. Mike told him his life was so terrible there was no reason for him to live. He admitted he wanted to kill himself, but he made Charlie promise to keep the secret.

But as the day went by, and Charlie was home with his family, he realized he couldn't keep it to himself. He knew he would be taking the chance of making Mike very angry. He knew, too, that he would be breaking his word to his friend. But he also decided that he'd rather have an angry friend than no friend at all. He knew that he had to tell somebody, or Mike could die.

"I told my dad," Charlie remembers. "I went into the kitchen and started crying. He got scared, really pale. He grabbed his coat and went over to Mike's. Later on when he came home, he said Mike would probably be okay, but he needed some help getting better. Mike's mom and dad said Mike would need to talk to a psychologist to figure out how to handle the

Many schools show films that remove the fantasy and mystery surrounding death.

stress and pressures in his life.

"I wasn't really sure what to expect the next time I saw Mike. I didn't know if he'd be mad at me for breaking my word. He started out very angry, but we're friends now. I know I did the right thing. Some secrets should never be kept."

OTHER WAYS TO HELP

Being a friend can be a big responsibility, especially if your friend is depressed or troubled in other ways. Psychologists say there are a few important rules to remember when you feel that a friend is thinking about suicide.

One mistake some people make is to try to talk the friend out of it—to tell her things aren't so bad. A suicidal teen obviously thinks things are bad, or she wouldn't be considering suicide. Treating her as though she were over-reacting would probably make her feel like more of a failure.

It's important to be a good listener. Sometimes by listening we show that we care how a friend feels. We don't need to "cheer up" our friend, or give a lecture, or argue with him. Communication, or lack of it, is one reason teens are at risk in the first place. A caring, non-judging friend can make all the difference in the world!

If you think a friend is in danger of killing himself,

It's important to listen to friends who want to talk about their feelings.

HIGH SCHOO
Understanding the World

it's important to stay with him until you can get help. If an adult is not around, call a suicide-prevention hotline. There are trained people working every day of the year, 24 hours a day, who can help.

THE WARNING SIGNS OF SUICIDE

1. Talking or thinking a lot about suicide or death.
2. Changes in eating or sleeping habits (usually a suicidal teen takes no interest in food and sleeps quite a bit more than normal).
3. Giving away valuable possessions without reason.
4. Withdrawing from family and friends.
5. Taking unnecessary risks, such as driving recklessly.
6. Drug or alcohol abuse (the teen who needs to feel good or different may be showing that his or her life is unhappy the way it is).
7. Depression that seems to go on longer than a normal mood swing (as mentioned earlier, depression is common, but prolonged periods of depression are not).

Remember that these seven signs are only a guide. There may be other kinds of behavior not on this list

A caring, non-judging friend can really help a depressed or angry teen.

that makes you worried about a friend. If you think someone you know fits into one or more of these categories, or appears to be at risk in some other way, talk to an adult. You may be saving a life!

A FINAL THOUGHT

It's possible, though, that no matter how hard we try, or how much we care, someone we know could commit suicide. As one psychiatrist tells her teenaged patients, "If you're hell-bent on killing yourself, I probably cannot stop you. I care, but I can't watch over you 24 hours a day."

One of the tragedies of teen suicide is the guilt and sadness of those left behind. They ask themselves if there was some clue they missed, some remark they didn't hear. Parents and friends go over and over the events of the day of the suicide, trying to understand what happened. Often, there will be nothing out of the ordinary.

But the grief the family feels is enormous. The hurt and sadness will never really go away, but hopefully the family will be able to find some comfort by talking together about their pain. Open and honest conversation, even when it didn't really happen before the suicide, is crucial if the family is to survive.

FOR MORE INFORMATION

For more information about teen suicide, write to:

The Youth Rescue Fund
3575 Cahuenga Blvd. West
Suite 255
Los Angeles, CA 90068

GLOSSARY/INDEX

ADOLESCENCE 13—*The teenage years, the time between childhood and adulthood.*
ANOREXIA NERVOSA 26—*An eating disorder suffered by some troubled teenagers. An anorectic teen slowly starves to death, unless he or she receives help.*
AT-RISK 16, 21, 24, 27, 33, 34—*A teen who has a dangerous combination of emotions that may indicate suicidal behavior.*
CENTER 18—*Those things in our lives that we always depend on.*
CONDITIONAL LOVE 29—*A type of pressure in which the person feels that he or she can only be loved if successful.*
EXAMINATION HELLS 31—*Stressful testing periods in Japanese schools.*
HARA-KIRI 9—*A form of suicide honored in Japan for centuries.*
MASK 24—*To cover up, to hide.*
PEER GROUP 19—*Friends one's own age. A peer group is especially important to teenagers.*
PSYCHIATRIST 10, 31, 32, 43—*A doctor who deals with emotional and mental illnesses.*
PSYCHOLOGIST 15, 19, 39, 40—*A person who studies human behavior.*

GLOSSARY/INDEX

SELF-ESTEEM 24, 27, 28, 29—*How we feel about ourselves.*
SUTTEE 9—*An old custom in Hindu society that urged a woman to kill herself when her husband died.*

10.40